082-1986)

Essential Poets 48

Jean-Paul Daoust

Black Diva
(Selected Poems: 1982-1986)

*Translated from the French
by Daniel Sloate
With a Preface by André Roy*

Guernica

Montreal, 1991

Antonio D'Alfonso, publisher and editor
Guernica Editions Inc.
P.O. Box 633, Station N.D.G.
Montreal (Quebec), Canada H4A 3R1

Legal Deposit — 4th Quarter.
Bibliothèque nationale du Québec.
National Library of Canada.

Canadian Cataloguing in Publication Data
Daoust, Jean-Paul
Black Diva: poems, 1982-1986
(Essential Poets; 48)
Translation of selections from various books of poetry by the author.
ISBN 0-920717-54-3
I. Sloate, Daniel. II. Title. III. Series.
PS8557.A591A27 1990 C841'.54 C90-090340-6
PQ3919.2.D36A27 1990

Contents

Preface

Jean-Paul Daoust always goes out with his 500 watts, bites into the phone, spirals from one place to another, a glass of champagne in his hand like a pink flamingo, mopes around, changes places, so what else is new, is scared of Electroluxes and jealousy, says bye bye to one poem after another; it's nighttime in Montreal like an odyssey, hearts change their surroundings, their looks, their letters at the Ritz and its impulses; what's on the agenda? The future, the rage of living, music, Florida and Bangkok, love's disaster in the April sky riddled with UFO's, in short with the barbaric routine of every day. Jean-Paul Daoust is starving, goes out to better stay inside himself, he is sick with desire in this city where brains collide like buses, yes sick with the desire to read this city in you when death is always so alert. With neon lights in his hair Jean-Paul Daoust takes off his mask, grimaces, winks, cruises, has fun at the Beaux Esprits but on St. Catherine too, and on St. Lawrence; city, oh city, epic, delirious like a tango, new wave, rock, reggae, with a beauty that droops under its own weight (maybe since with its pair of pink lips it always sleeps with one eye open). Jean-Paul Daoust, it's true, puts on heavy make-up like trees with false eyelashes, it's true, he's tender so tender, an alcoholic in his writing, he's alone and he screams, his member elsewhere but where? In Bahia? I can see him touching someone, his body agitated, freaking out, brimming over, the whites of his eyes even whiter on the edge of the blue swimming pool, tired, expecting what? Love with his heart that's blink-blinking, his eyes full of plumes. Jean-Paul Daoust laughs, cries, desires, somersaults so he won't get dizzy, won't hear all that blond thunder; his member is tattooed blue like mine, he sheathes his claws, picks up his sequins, he's flammable, I remember his heart goes tilt; words are synthetic hieroglyphs, they fall like tears, like distracted water lilies; you'd like to be happy with the guy. Jean-Paul Daoust: has he stopped his typewriter? Is he frantic, down, drugged, all made up on St. Denis street some boring Sunday afternoon? He thinks he's Mae West, Frankenstein, Dracula, King Tut, Rita Hayworth, King Kong, Esther Williams in the tropics, in Asia, on Broadway just for the fun of it, with sparkles on his lips. Jean-Paul Daoust likes a lot of people and things and some of them are: Bette Davis, Lucien Francoeur, Walt Disney, Italian mini-bathing suits, the basso nova, Las Vegas, snort, Planter's punch in the shade of the palm trees, Monopoly, credit cards and the queens at the Truxx. Me too.

André Roy

Eyes of the Desert

A blue valentine
Full of broken bottles
That the liver spews into filthy sinks
In welfare apartments
Scream my guts out
The shock of my tongue lolling like a necktie
The acid rock of the eardrum
Deflower my brain
Not laugh and pop the braces on my teeth
Prowl clad in pink in the dark
Puncture those desert eyes
The hair
Hysterical belts
The voice backing off
Hands that flatten out
Fingernails like dead fish eyes
Epic effort to lift the pinkie
Contemptuous flesh of life's corpse
Experiments on the heart's mirages
The weatherbeaten sign at the oasis
Sorry we're closed
Have fun with no coke
Can it be those lips that are touching
The moon is rubbing its black cheek against the sun
The surreal images in a sorrow's culture
The evening belongs only to Las Vegas
The window on the alley filthier than a neglected sore
These long nights with their deserted highways
In search of accidents
Tortures
Burns
Deserts have instant gestures of eternity
Just a lot of sand
Hard solid blond sand
Whips in the ultimate music of sandstorms
You'll die if you don't protect yourself

Silly passports
No one believes in them anymore
Desert fevers
Hysterical camels
Deep in hungry seas
The cinema's caravan
The air wrinkles with sere sounds
Fruit crumbles like snakeskin
New York snaps its skyscrapers like matches
The howling of cavernous skulls
The desert has wrinkles that terrify Hollywood
A footstep is only an ephemeral swim
A useless obstacle
A boring mirage
Here is where death preens himself
In full sunlight
The sand and its steel reflections
The eyes burnt to a crisp in fierce reflections
Well, wouldn't you like a cold bottle of champagne
The desert like an overdose of madness
The eyes open their dams in vain
The silk of the nostrils can't withstand it
The throat is nothing but a furnace
The cancer of the moment
At noon in the desert there's a shower of suicides
Of petrified nightmares
Of broken loves
The heart
This lonely hunter and all
Dries up
Vitrifies
Come and see for yourself
Eyes of plaster
The desert has stopped weeping
The blood with its bald waters
Can't you hear the music of the ruins

Jeering amidst the vultures' feet
Or is it a hyena
These dates recalling certain halts
Nothing but a crust
When the sand shifts it's the better to kill
That final pose on death's horizon
The telephone doesn't ring in the desert
The rough palm that slaps
Claws in the eyes
Lenses that shatter
Already the blood dries
The desert of the morning of the evening
Sun or no
Here the seasons don't change
The mummified heart
Tenderness
A ring not worn anymore by day or night
The face nothing more than a rifled pyramid
Just another violated valley
The desert groans on the banks of the Nile
It's rough and tough
Las Vegas like a standing mirror
Finely chiselled
Pleasure's refrain
Brutal but effective mirror
A voice full of crevasse-deep wrinkles
The eyes of the desert move before they die
Like a TV screen full of snow
Here the absurd is only a passing invention
La Callas still sings on these sealess beaches
A howl that eats like acid
This sun
This desert

1982

Egyptian Poem

I'll write a poem for you
In the Egyptian style
On your skin
Hieroglyphs of love
That our fingers will decipher
I'm going to mummify you
Wind you in wrappings
And kisses
Our careful ritual gestures
To keep you
In my eternity
I'll stretch you out
In the core of my heart
Where no one can go
Its beat is like music
To soothe you
To lull you
Love you
In the desert
Flooded with light
Our skin burning like sand
In the shade
The two of us
With our erections like obelisks of sacred light
Jealously guarded by the sphinx of love

1982

Solitude

Solitude. That blocks the eyes. Fatigue. And yet the desire. For passion. There where the *I* is most numerous. That stagnant state of the past. An *I* condemned. Another. Avalanche of black. Gestures of consolation are decapitated. Despair's hemorrhage. A strong poison to. Swallow. Last phase.

Solitude. That catapults toward nameless bodies. *A city is always full of them.* A pink cowboy. Who. Waits. With eyes like raw silk. That are paralyzed in mirages engulfing hysterical laughter. Make-up of the soul. But. We know that. *Face lifts* don't work on the heart. Solitude. Like a bitch you detest. But. That you tame. So she won't devour you. She takes us for one of her sick children.

Solitude. The *I* is bored. By. Your dinosaur smile. By beauty. When the *I* was WE. Is it illusion, just fabulating. Who knows. The diamond solitaire casts reflections of hate. Your full moon smile. Where the *I.* Lucky astronaut. Light. Eros in the Thanatos of the universe. And then. The fall. Into the void. The stars are plague carriers. And words that can't go on. And all that commits suicide at the bottom of the page.

Solitude. An *overdose* just by yourself. Too bad. In the body's computer, memory contemplates the gods of yore. On the aging screen of the skin appears an aging star. Like in a silent film. What raving. Fingernails get chewed like *popcorn.* While. The brain hallucinates. *Give me a break man. I'm dying.* But it all goes on anyway.

Solitude. Pacing up and down my neurons. Broken-down streets. An evening of acid rain. In the city. The skin makes a leap forward. And breaks. Wrinkles. The hair falls. Old age. Mirror of death.

Solitude. Its spines. Cactus. In the opaque desert of life. *Everyone is afraid of a lonely writer.* What a *flop.*

Solitude. Each word kamikazes in its sentence. That no one holds on to. A feather undone from an angel's flight. Twirling in the hell of its fall. Like a *rock star.* Totally drugged. Washed up. Who's watching an old *hit parade* from the past. When she was at the top. But. As each sunset is peopled with jets flying in unison. That rise. But. *Crash at first sight.*

Solitude. Picking up garbage. Refuse-dump body. But of course. The brain looks like an intestine. And vice-versa. *Born for hell.* Live. On a credit card. Stolen. Full. *Blue millionaire.* Solitude. A bag-lady. Disfigured. By all those blows. Words vanish. Anemic.

Solitude. Climbing into the heart. A varicose vein ladder. A diabolical flood. *Purple rain.* Where the heart suffocates. The brain has blown up its dams. *Black out* for planet Body. The astral body. Extinguished. The ugly trees of March. Their turtle skin. In a nuclear sky. Where presidents travel. Popes. *Apocalypse time.* But. The bodies. Like rats. Making love in the sewers. Where the heart of slum city is rotting.

Solitude. But. The most beautiful love poems are written in a bed. That the skin remembers for a while. Look at that skin. Read what's written on it. Don't censure anything. Try. Read it over again. Maybe. The beautiful moments it's lived. Tremble. When seeing. The passion of all those lips. That came there to drink. But. I'd be hijacked. Spied on. By paper James Bonds.

Solitude. Now. Alone. Like the tongue. A red carpet. Useless. But *I'm generous and I got style.* My fingernails in my mouth. Safety vaults. For caresses.

Empty. Pillaged. Like tombs in the burning desert. *Wanna love before we die.* Should do it. But the dead. Alone. Who smell of death.

Solitude. It would take a miracle. To change this lyrical text. Into a luminous postcard. And this city. Crouched on the banks of the river. Like a crocodile. With fresh teeth. The *I* never thought it could go so far into. Solitude. Memories with their scent of orchids. The heart feeds its parasites well.

Solitude. Smearing the skin of my soul. Its cold kiss. Panic. Eyes. Modesty. Eyelids. That close. Curtains. Of skin. On an opera. Solitary. Night. Distress. Of dawn. Arriving in its make-up. Make a drink. To fill. The grey hour. But. Solitude. As someone once said in a song. To the point of screaming. Lips open up like Marilyn's legs. In the flash of teeth all the world's sadness dances.

Solitude. Like a forgotten *cover girl.* Take your face in your hands. Because they are the last reservoir of caresses left. Fingers. Stems for faded flowers. Their worn out eyes. But. This void. Between the trembling fingers. Flags of. Solitude.

Solitude. Of the body. Moving forward. Like a parade float moving through a nameless crowd. Put make-up on my eyes. Black make-up. The better to show off my night. The sudden urge to laugh. At all that. The heart plunges into another glass. Alcohol. Sacred river wherein the heart purifies its pain. You cheer yourself up as best you can. Words. Ashes. On the beach. Grains of sand. In the Sahara of a life. Lips collapse on their porcelain rocks. Exhausted. Starving. *Nothing. Except. ME.* No one. And the body continues its voyage through the time of others. The sounds of conversations. *Cheap* operas. The *I* moves amidst its phantoms. The *I* clings to words. Final madness. The world is an unhappy place. Poetry freaks out.

Solitude. Of a winter. That's endless. Do the dead. The dead. Do they speak of the living. Of this new *mal de vivre*. That the dandies of this age parade before all. Decors change. Like the waves. Of a single sea. Suns of ebony. And. Limbo. Coma. And. Solitude. Blind. Deaf. Mute.

Solitude. Paralyzing the text. Photographed by a tourist *I*. Who will soon be knifed by the pain of words. *Life goes on. Not ME*. And the *I* goes into exile in a hotel of ice. Dreams don't grow anymore. As-phalted over. The indifference of others. Him. The eye harpoons him. In vain. *Moby Dick rides again*. And all the morons round about. *Jellyfishes*. A writer is fed up. Gets up. Goes and gets himself another drink. And leaves the machine. All alone.

Solitude. Like a panther. That's hunting. In the city. Where Tarzan is. Those skyscrapers. Phos-phorescent baobabs. That the heart climbs. From up there it can fling itself. The city. *A jam session of lonely hearts*. Jets overhead. Mechanical insects. Taxis below. Roaring when called. Momentarily. But. Spiders spin in people's eyes the next *delirium tremens*. *Paradise is an invention of a mad genius*. Illusions. Physical though. Give up trying to make sense of it all. And. The ring. Alone. On the finger. Alone.

Solitude. That laughs. Fierce. Words. A caravan of them. The skin. In the sun. Storm. Over the cos-metic being. Carnage. Death casts his long shadow. Over the *suntan*. Solitude. Turning in circles. Like an electron. The pulverized smile. Slides over the eye's black screen. *Nobody. Loves. ME*. Enough material to write a text.

Solitude. Insatiable vampire. Each and every life gives its blood. And when the eyes turn inward they see nothing but madness. Alone. Like a Vestal Virgin. Guarding the temple of boredom. And there. No one prays.

Solitude. *No return.* No port of call. Just the mirages that the heart has consented to keep. Just a little game. Solitude plays games. Too. Loser takes all. Words. Jewels she gives herself. Luxury. She buys it. But at what a price. Every life pays into it. Always a loser.

Solitude. The *I.* Bang of a fist. On the concrete of cities. But her *buildings.* So much the *star.* Behind dark glasses. But there is nothing sadder than the end of a *star. Have you seen Bette Davis lately?*

Solitude. It's the cry of the stars. Styles. Who programs the computers. The verdigris of the screen. That can't imagine another thing. Other than the void. The brain explodes. In the absoluteness of its distress. *Tilt.*

Solitude. The cat. White. In my arms. Lamenting. Alone. What tormented spirit possesses her. Men have the eyes of volcanoes that children are sacrificed in. But. The *I* can't stand it anymore. Solitude is a light that shines on nothing but the void. And the blank space between these words. Solitary.

Solitude.

You feel so alone in the midst of words when the book is closed.

1985

Magic Boys

I have luminous nights. Where bold bodies shine. Their quick kisses. Startling nights. *And my life is a full moon affair. Like your smile.* My pharaoh eyes. But my hands are aging. On skins increasingly alert. My hands are limousines that are driving down DEAD ENDS. I have a Los Angeles face. Earthquakes. *More to come. Love me with all your skin, you dirty snake.* Beside you a rose is just an ordinary miracle. *And the leaves of autumn. The lips of death.* But tonight I'm miserable. *Ready to leave this planet.* These landscapes I know backwards and forwards where the suns set. My hands are drying out. Coral deprived of its seahorses. Where have you gone. *Help me. Someone please help me. It's a rock 'n'roll prayer. But there's no God.* I need an angel with perfumed fur. His feathers fallen down my neck. Love you. Love you. Love you. Fingers don't move fast enough as they try to feel that ephemeral dazzle when your skin drives me crazy. I'm screaming because you kissed me and that was what I wanted. Till I'm drunk from it. Till I die from it.

Everything has an end — even death, do you understand?

EVERYTHING HAS AN END — EVEN DEATH.

Now let's talk. The better to see the mirror that reflects startling images back to us. *How amazing. But I don't know you. And you?* Your powerful eyes. The Vatican shies away. Moscow gives up. The Pentagon forgets. *When you're powerful. It beats God.*

But I'll let your skin tell me other tales.

His cattleya eyes. When he puckers his festive lips. His teeth are full mirrors. Has to do with porcelain too. Who boldly dared frame his bold body. Every gesture like a sheaf of light. Fingers have smiles that lovers alone detect. Has to do with soaring. A skin is a fascinating land. When lips sculpture the heart. *It's a smile. For Eternity*. Eyelashes have plumes. You like a sun in my eyes. Your Jamaica body. The surging. Into time. Our lives. His candour when he turns toward me. Who's watching him. His eyes are two wings of bronze. His terrace smile. Where I leisurely drink my pink champagne. The heart at last rends its shell. Free as Tarzan among the vines *sniffing* an orchid. Question. The petals answer. *He loves me he loves me not he loves me*. Our resourceful bodies. Dancing. *All night*.

He's making love right this minute. I know. With someone else. What can I do about it. Except stare at this motionless fog where the evening is vanishing. His silence. This burning moment that's consuming me. Don't panic. WHATEVER YOU DO. Otherwise disaster time. Wait. For it to be over. For him to come back to me. For him to want me. Plant my teeth in his neck to scare his blood. Clutch his hair. My claws unsheathed. Another swan is dying. May apocalyptic fury be celebrated on our tongues. I walk delicately through the apartment. I explode at the least squabble. I'm an atomic bomb. Crazy crippled telephone there. Old thing. Deaf. Dumb. If he were here obviously everything would be just fine. Obviously. I'd be bitchy to him though. Like an *extra large all dressed* pizza with a double order of anchovies a *Chinese dinner for three* five St-Hubert BBQ chickens obscene telephone calls a telegram singing: *Fuck you. Fuck you. Fuck you. Fuck you. Fuck you. Fuck you. Fuck you. Fuck you.* But my body is eating the silence. Barely moving except to grab a rum and coke. And put it down like a piece of ebony. Very chic, I don't even wipe away a tear that starts down my face. Lava. A new wrinkle. Because of him. The TV is on. I can hear it buzzing. America and its mechanical presence. I'm so anxious for him to come home so we can both laugh. At us. The hesitation before the first kiss. More tears will follow. The heart is in eruption. His transparent dross. He really is making love to someone else. Maybe he's in love with him. Maybe not. And when he comes back he'll have that champagne smile of his. He'll bury his lying eyes in my skin. But he'll come back. Until then all I can do is wait. Everybody's lived through what I'm going through. So what's the matter except my pain. More poems are stuck in my throat. It's not that I'm afraid of comparisons. *I know who I am.* But him. So far away suddenly. Perilous sirens sing in my tears. Sad eruptions from the eyes. The WE is foundering. Night. A punctured eye. But there's no big deal. He's just making love with another guy. My words are submerged in tears. Angels with damp wings can't fly. Alone. My heart as it writes screeches like fingernails on a blackboard. The picture is empty. Eyes blaze in the storm. And the day is rising. Its crooked smile. And those immaculate sheets. Like a shroud around a death-stricken heart. Mummified.

It's snowing. Words. The page. Passive.
I've always loved you.
My skin. Deserted beach. Where I grow sand roses.
Castles as bright as your eyes.
I've always loved you.
Your hands. Made for picking the rarest of flowers.
Your fingers folding. On my lips your greedy tongue
gathers words.
I've always loved you.
It's snowing. Suns. You're beautiful. Like a Viking on
his drakkar.
En route for his conquest.
I've always loved you.
In your Himalaya arms. I'm playing. The yeti.
Don't you remember.
I'm Ramses II.
I'm building crystal pyramids for you.
I'm your magician.
I've always loved you.
Like the spring loves the swallows in the sky.
I've always loved you.
My angel with heart of jade.

Novels are needed to depict all that. Poems to stigmatize those loves. Other trophy texts for the trembling flesh. I wear my skin like a new alphabet to be deciphered. Us. Accomplices at last.

Oh yes, we are magic boys.

These words in your ears attentive at last to our becoming. Our excitement. Our lives on vacation. For ever. I'm dreaming. Wide awake. But I dare to give in to the drive to want to be happy. Whereas all around me is fascism. Its rotten codes. Tortures. So love me more. This text where I survive as though in a hothouse. I'm afraid. The medieval fortress. Haunted. Its dungeons. I'm being pushed into the battle when I'm trying to work in my alchemist's lab.

I'm a sorcerer. My powers will make the magic boys arrive. At last.

I don't want to be burnt again.

Now is the time when extraordinary guys discuss their becoming.

Their caresses. Their starred fingers.

Their tragic skin. Daring to hope.

Now is the time of the magic boys.

1986

The Sleeping Angel

I'm watching him as he sleeps. His skin, relaxed. Beautiful angel. His eyes sheltered. In their enchanted settings. I'm watching him as he sleeps. His skin lying there. Trustingly. I put out a finger. And move it about. Over his eyelids. Their silk. I feel his eyes smiling. Calmly. I write words with my fingertip. Tender words. That I don't dare say to him. I'm frightened when he's afraid. Sweat. My desire like misty rain. I'm restraining myself. So I don't pounce on him. Like a tiger. But. I retract my nails. So I can stroke his sleeping body. His nice soft fur, so soft. Feathers. I'm watching him as he sleeps. I shiver. What if he decides to leave. Or get out of bed. Or spread his wings. And fly away. My heart stops. Stops dead. Total despair. Black. Cold. My finger stops writing. I'd like him to catch these words with his lips. I'm hesitating. Should I go on. Only he knows. Me. I want him. He knows that. I'm watching him as he sleeps. In the pearl-grey morning. Lying on the bed. In all his glory. A blue-blooded angel. While he's asleep. Is he pretending? I'm weaving a net around him. Around us. My finger is now in his curls. Amber curls. But what I'm really staring at is his lips. Incredibly beautiful lips. Delicate. But strong. Serious. Maddening. That's where he's hiding. I'm venturing into his lair. With my fingertips. Just the tips. Velvet tips. I know he's worried. But I'm doing it anyway. No one has ventured there before me. I know that. But I want him to know that I'm an angel. Just like him. And that I love him. His lips are opening. Is it for a kiss. Or to bite. No reason for him to be defensive. There's no one attacking him. My lips are close to his. Ready to take them. To touch them. To rock them. I didn't know he was so miserable. So fragile. And so decided at the same time. I'm waiting. For him to move. He's opening his eyes. I'm caught. In the act.

Like a thief. Of images. He's looking at me. He doesn't condemn me but. Maybe a reproach. I'm not moving. I'm terrified. Like a child on the brink of a lie. He puts out his hand and it frightens me to death. But he places his hand on my shoulder. As though to console me. He wants me to go to sleep. But does he realize what state I'm in. How insane I am. And suddenly I'm the one who's snared in his arms. I struggle. But I have a feeling he's going to win. I remove my fingers from his hair. The way you remove an orchid from the jungle. But I loved playing the parasite. I imagine the two of us in the sea. In the waves. In the sunlight. The salt I lick off his skin. As the blue of the sky veers and falls like a gigantic curtain so we can see the stars dancing. The moon. The universal goddess. And him. More lavish than all the lavish spectacles in the world. True. I'm sleeping. With him. And I'm dreaming. What about him? I want him to speak to me. To take me with him to his country. I've glimpsed incredible landscapes. Insane. There are exotic gardens in his eyes. In his eyes where it's always summer. And his body's performances absolutely stun me. Solitude crumbles away to dust. An expired idol. He has changed my outlook on life. Put a stop to time. That sleeps with him. I hold back my tears. My cries. My desire crazed and wild. But. One movement and he catches hold of me. The shock of affection. Again. In his lips I'd sign any and all pacts. And I'd give my soul to the devil with a laugh on my lips. *How can I sell something that I don't have anymore.* I'd change myself into a fierce dragon and shield his body from any attacker. *Love isn't a joke.* When I move my lips up and down his body it makes incredible music. Music of the angels, you might say. He can hear it too. I pile up postcards on his back. Fragile gifts. I can't get enough of his kisses. Caress after caress after caress.

The wild country he takes me to. Where he has never dared take anyone else before. I feel like a barbarian. I'm looking at him. I can see he's surprised at having come so far. Like being in a new land. Both of us amazed to see that it really does exist. Worried too. Nervous as two angels flying in a magnificent but unknown sky. With unhappiness lying in ashes somewhere else. In forgotten places. His California face. Where I'm a traveller. As blissfully happy as a movie star. His arms are as sophisticated as the Ritz. With its panelled rooms. Its sparkling afternoons. Its *far-niente*. At times his gestures are unexpected. And surprise even him. When he moves closer to kiss me. When his jeans explode before my eyes. The heart clings. To his skin. And falls off with a song. Sublime diva in a made-to-measure opera. Every passion unleashed. Irresistably modern. I'm watching him as he sleeps. My amazement at his being there. So close. His pores are breathing. Like flowers. My fingers are restless. And write love letters to every part of his body. To tell him things you're not supposed to say. Too bad. I can't help dropping messages all over his skin. Little multi-coloured parachutes. Invasion. His eyes roll in their sockets like certain sunsets. Under closed eyelids. On mornings of cool light. How to make him happy. How to destroy his defences. So I can talk to him about happiness. About our being together. Just the two of us. In a bed where our members are in love with each other. Members of the same sex. *So what.* I'm watching him as he sleeps. Like a guy. In love. He's sleeping. One arm is folded over his head. As though buried in a sheaf of nervous plumes. Waging war is out of the question here. Or being the other guy's nazi. Or his shark. My lips continue their promenade along his skin. On his neck. And they sow blazing suns there. To chase away his shadows. His cold nights. Write him what he's afraid to hear. But what he knows. I don't want to be cast among the nameless. Their petty limbo. I want to take him to a hundred Tahiti lives. Let newer New Yorks be built. And cathedrals. Their flamboyant crystals. I want him to love me. I want him to fall into my arms. Nervous. Excited. And I want him to give himself to me. AT LAST. I want him to shed his skin. And leave the old husk to scavenger birds. My finger touches his new skin. Proud. And his whole body turns its petals toward love. I have images in my hands. That I gather from his skin's offering. Yes I'm watching him as he sleeps. And all the images I've gathered I spread out before me. And gaze intently at them. Before making a sumptuous bouquet that I'll hand to him when he wakes up. And the more I harvest the more his hardy skin yields. He is an incredibly rich angel. I succumb to the madness. Of this angel ready for anything. I'm watching him as he sleeps. Like a sailing ship riding at anchor. Peaceful. Not a single wrinkle on the surface of the air. Music. Tam-tam. The heart proclaims the glad tidings. *Me and him. The angels of love.* So close. He's sleeping. And my fingers are dreaming. He's a beach that no one has seen. I discover its fine sand. Almond. His eyes. Two mahogany suns. I soar into the sky as I once did in the gulf of Siam. But that skyscape was empty. Now the sky has a face. And the heart is a dazed astronaut. The impetuous beauty of that universe. Yes, I mean yours. Where I'm floating. Free. Happy. And I want to show you other flights. I know your body. Intelligent. Your clever hands. Your violent desire. So come here and we'll take off. I stretch out my fingers. Gazelles in the savanna of your hair. You. You're sleeping. Fabulous beast. And I feel so good. Protected. My fingers are dancing on your skin. And you're amused to see me acting so crazy. You make fun of me a little. To conceal how you feel. You look around you. But there's no one there. No one. Except US. So you take a risk. Your fingers dance with my fingers. And your skin and mine stage a ballet with very moving choreography. You grow tender. And you spread your big body like a fan with disturbing designs. I'm watching him as he sleeps. The angel with the bountiful body. I withdraw my fingers. Except for one. That glides over his forehead. Comes back to his eyes. Your eyelid trembles. Slightly. Then calms down. And I see that your eyes agree. In harmony. With our desire. For EACH OTHER. And my finger continues its glide along your nose. A little fall and it's on your lips. Soft carpet. But with passion for weave. My finger catches. On your breathing. Your body murmurs. But doesn't move. My finger continues downward. Along the chin. The neck. And I can't hold back anymore. My lips curl around your skin. And I start to purr. Happiest of cats. I'm listening to you as you sleep. I'm stalking your dreams. I close my eyes. Like yours are. And I can see you. You were expecting me. And we soar. Into the blue of the air. Two angels. AT LAST. Happy.

1986

To Be Happy

To be happy
I can say
That I've applied make-up
To the void
Put more teeth in smiles
Than the smiles could contain
In the heart
Enough energy to blow up NASA
And all the alcohol in my veins
Just an immense pain
To solitude
To loves that have collapsed
Ah, the domestic disasters
My poor life
To the beat of *what's going on*
I've wandered from mouth to mouth
I've kissed teeth true and false
I did everything to be happy
I was supposed to do
But in vain
The formula has not yet been found
At every real wound
The heart bursts
Like an audience
The aorta pops
Because the heart is on a stage
That collapses
To be happy
I could tell you things
That'd send shivers through you
Because
But there goes the heart
Ensconced in a fake galaxy
The police catch up to me
And kill me
Because to be happy

You always do things
That make you tremble all over

1986

By the Same Author

Oui, cher (1976)

Chaises longues (1977)

Portrait d'intérieur (1981)

Poèmes de Babylone (1982)

Black Diva (1983)

Taxi (1984)

Soleils d'acajou (1984)

La peau du coeur et son opéra (1985)

Dimanche après-midi (1985)

Du Dandysme (1986)

Les garçons magiques (1986)

Suite contemporaine (1987)

Printed by
Ateliers Graphiques Marc Veilleux Inc.
Cap-Saint-Ignace Qué.
in May 1991